Super Safari

Level 3

Student's Book

Herbert Puchta ● **Günter Gerngross** ● **Peter Lewis-Jones**

CAMBRIDGE
UNIVERSITY PRESS

Map of the book

Hello! (pages 4–7)

Vocabulary	Grammar
Hello! What's your name? I'm ...	red, blue, green, orange, purple, yellow

▶ **Song:** What's your name?

① My classroom (pages 8–15)

Vocabulary	Vocabulary 2	Story and value	CLIL	Thinking skills
pencil, chair, bag, eraser, book, desk	seven, eight, nine, ten	**The pencil** Lending	Actions at school	Categorizing

▶ **Total physical response:** Stand up. Put your bag on your desk. Sit down. Open your book. Pick up your pencil. Close your book.　▶ **Song:** In the classroom

② My family (pages 16–23)

Vocabulary	Grammar	Story and value	CLIL	Thinking skills
grandpa, grandma, mom, dad, sister, brother	This is my (brother).	**The sandwiches** Sharing	Familiy trees	Organizing information

▶ **Total physical response:** Open the door. Say hello to your mom. Sit down. What's that? Stand up. It's a sandwich.　▶ **Song:** We're the Royal family!

③ My face (pages 24–31)

Vocabulary	Grammar	Story and value	CLIL	Thinking skills
eyes, ears, nose, face, teeth, mouth	I'm / You're (angry / happy / sad / scared).	**The monster** Being nice to friends	Music and feelings	Interpreting feelings

▶ **Total physical response:** Close your eyes. Put out your hands. What is it? Open your eyes. A present! You're happy! Give your friend a hug.　▶ **Song:** Hey, little clown

④ My toys (pages 32–39)

Vocabulary	Grammar	Story and value	CLIL	Thinking skills
ball, kite, jump rope, teddy bear, doll, plane	I have a (ball).	**The ball** Working together	Playing outside	Remembering sequences

▶ **Total physical response:** Throw the ball. Look at the ball. Throw the jump rope. Catch the ball. Bounce the ball. Put the ball in your bag.　▶ **Song:** I don't have a kite

⑤ My house (pages 40–47)

Vocabulary	Grammar	Story and value	CLIL	Thinking skills
bathtub, cabinet, bed, couch, table, armchair	The (doll) is (in / on / under) the (cabinet).	*The cap* Listening to people	Homes	Planning and making

▶ **Total physical response:** Where's the cat? Listen. Look on the couch. Look under the table. No, it isn't there. Oh, look! It's in the cabinet! | ▶ **Song:** Put your toys away!

⑥ On the farm (pages 48–55)

Vocabulary	Grammar	Story and value	CLIL	Thinking skills
cat, horse, cow, dog, rabbit, sheep	My favorite (color) is (orange).	*I like your colors!* Paying compliments	Where animals live	Categorizing

▶ **Total physical response:** Sniff like a rabbit. Eat like a rabbit. Look! A dog! Hop, rabbit, hop! Run, dog, run! Hide, rabbit, hide! | ▶ **Song:** The animal boogie

⑦ I'm hungry! (pages 56–63)

Vocabulary	Grammar	Story and value	CLIL	Thinking skills
carrots, sausages, apples, cakes, ice cream, fries	I like / don't like (carrots).	*Cakes and ice cream* Eating sensibly	Where food comes from	Organizing information

▶ **Total physical response:** Smell. What's that smell? You're hungry. Go into the kitchen. Listen. Look – fries! Take one. Eat the fry. You like fries. Yummy! | ▶ **Song:** I don't like fries

⑧ All aboard! (pages 64–71)

Vocabulary	Grammar	Story and value	CLIL	Thinking skills
boat, train, car, scooter, bus, bike	I'm / You're (riding) a (bike).	*Oh, what fun!* Saying *thank you*	Shape pictures	Focusing on detail

▶ **Total physical response:** You're flying your plane. There's a café under the plane. Land your plane. Get out and go to the café. Ask for lots of ice cream. Yummy! | ▶ **Song:** We're having fun!

⑨ Party clothes (pages 72–79)

Vocabulary	Grammar	Story and value	CLIL	Thinking skills
hat, belt, boots, shirt, button, shoes	Let's have (cookies / chips / salad / candy).	*Nice work!* Cleaning up	Our clothes	Recognizing numbers

▶ **Total physical response:** Walk home. Open the door. Surprise! It's a party! Hooray! Put on your party hat. Eat cakes. Yummy! Dance with your friends | ▶ **Song:** Oh, what a wonderful party!

⑩ Phonics (pages 85–94)

Unit 1: "r" red, rabbit	Unit 2: "f" fish, family	Unit 3: "h" happy, hat	Unit 4: "g" dog, dig	Unit 5: "y" yellow, yogurt	Unit 6: "z" zebra, zoo	Unit 7: "c," "k" cat, king	Unit 8: "ng" singing, dancing	Unit 9: Alphabet

Chants pages 80–84   **Review** pages 90–95   **Cutouts:** 101–102   **Certificate:** 103   **Stickers:** End section

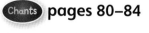   www.cambridge.org/supersafari/familyfun

3

Hello!

1 CD1 02 03 **Listen and sing.**

Listen and say the numbers and colors. Trace.

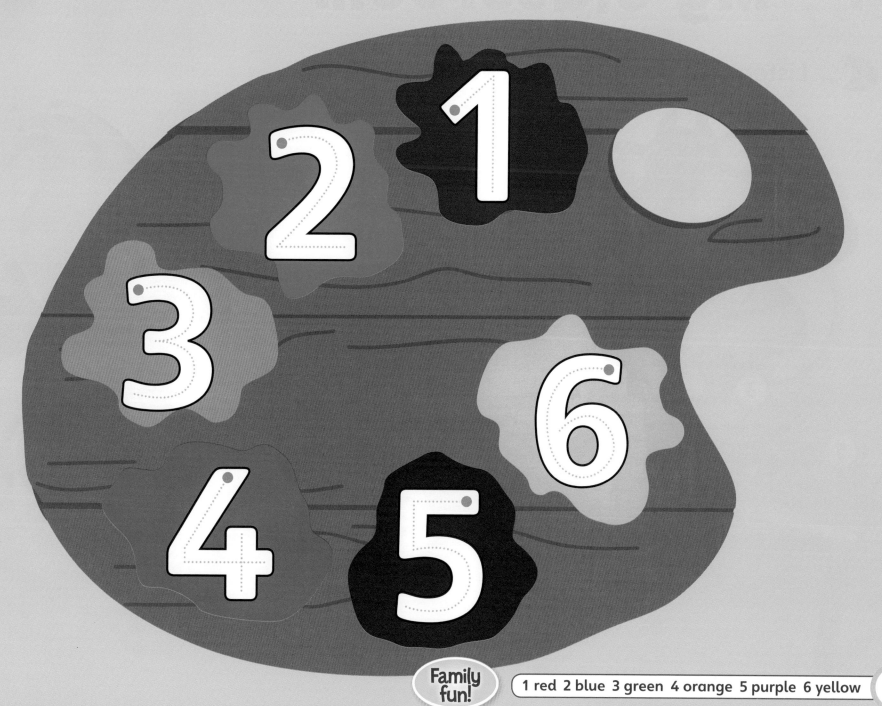

Family fun!

1 red 2 blue 3 green 4 orange 5 purple 6 yellow

1 My classroom

1 pencil 2 chair 3 bag 4 eraser 5 book 6 desk

Chant → page 80

2 CD1 09 **Listen and say the numbers. Trace.**

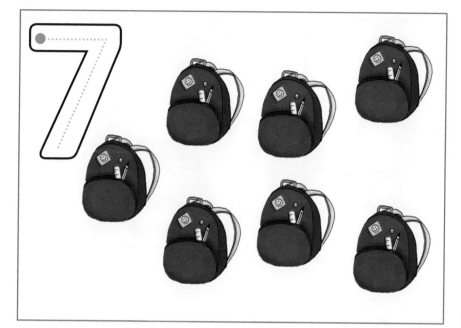

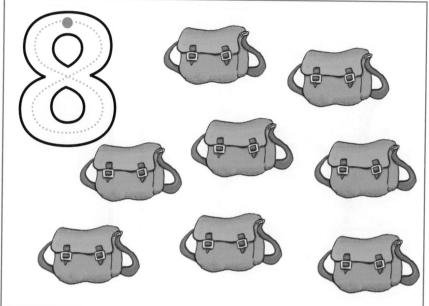

Listen and act. Listen and match.

1 **2** **3** **4** **5** **6**

Listen and sing.

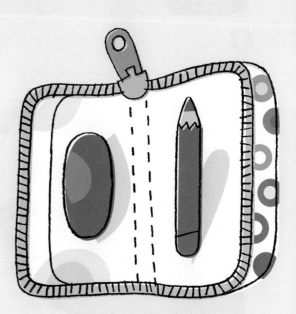

The pencil

Values

1

2

3

4

Actions at school

6 CD1 17 **Listen and say the words. Act it out.**

7 Think! **Think and color.**

1

2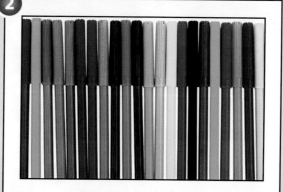

3

4

5

6

2 My family

1 CD1 20 **Listen and point. Say the words.**

1 grandpa 2 grandma 3 mom 4 dad 5 sister 6 brother

Chant → page 80

2 Listen and color. Say the sentences.

Family fun! This is my (brother). 17

3 **CD1 24 25** Listen and act. Listen and match.

1 **2** **3** **4** **5** **6**

Total physical response

4 CD1 26 27 Listen and sing.

The sandwiches

Family trees

 6 CD1 29 **Listen and stick.**

Sticker

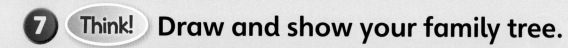

7 **Think!** Draw and show your family tree.

②

1 CD1 32 **Listen and point. Say the words.**

1 eyes 2 ears 3 nose 4 face 5 teeth 6 mouth

Chant → page 81

2 CD1 34 Sticker **Listen and say the sentences. Stick.**

1

2

3

4

Family fun!

I'm / You're (angry / happy / sad / scared).

25

Listen and act. Listen and match.

1 **2** **3** **4** **5** **6**

4 CD1 38 39 **Listen and sing.**

The monster

Family fun!

Value: Being nice to friends

Music and feelings

6 CD1 41 Listen and color. Say the instruments.

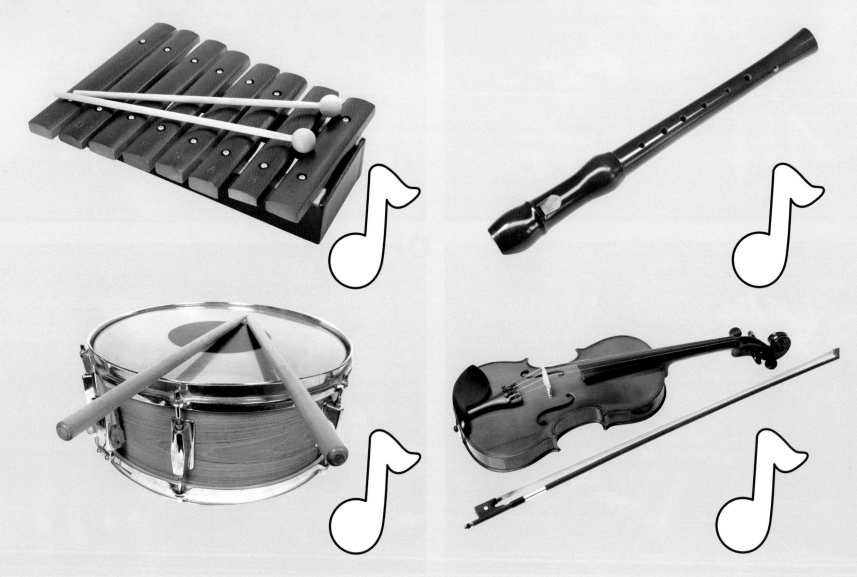

7 CD1 42 **Think!** **Listen and circle.**

1   2   3   4

1   2   3   4

1   2   3   4

1   2   3   4

Thinking skills: Interpreting feelings   **31**

4 My toys

1 CD1 45 Listen and point. Say the words.

1 ball

2 kite

4 teddy bear

3 jump rope

5 doll

6 plane

Chant → page 81

2 CD1 47 Listen and color. Say the sentences.

Family fun!

I have a (ball).

33

3 Listen and act. Listen and match.

1 **2** **3** **4** **5** **6**

4 CD1 50 51 Listen and sing.

The ball

1

2

3

4

Playing outside

1

2

3

4

7 CD1 55 56 **Think!** **Listen and color. Listen and act.**

Thinking skills: Remembering sequences **39**

5 My house

1 CD2 02 **Listen and point. Say the words.**

1 bathtub
2 cabinet
3 bed
4 couch
5 table
6 armchair

1 bathtub 2 cabinet 3 bed 4 couch 5 table 6 armchair

Chant → page 82

Listen and circle. Listen and answer.

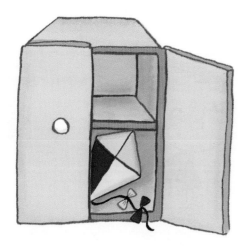 **1**

 **2**

 **3**

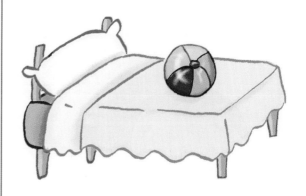

Family fun!

The (doll) is (in / on / under) the (cabinet). 41

Listen and act. Listen and match.

CD2 05 06

1 **2** **3** **4** **5** **6**

4 Listen and sing.

CD2
07 08

Family fun!

Singing for fun

43

The cap

Values

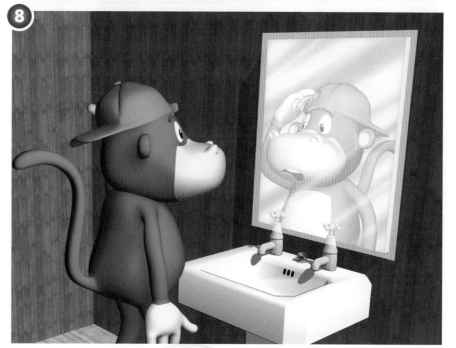

Family fun!

Value: Listening to people

Homes

6 CD2 11 Listen and say. Draw your home.

1

2

3

4

5

7 (Think!) **Choose a home and make it.**

Thinking skills: Planning and making   47

6 On the farm

1 CD2 14 Listen and point. Say the words.

1 cat

2 horse

3 cow

4 dog

5 rabbit

6 sheep

1 cat 2 horse 3 cow 4 dog 5 rabbit 6 sheep

Chant → page 82

2 Listen and circle. Say the sentences.

1

2

Family fun!

My favorite (color) is (orange). **49**

Listen and act. Listen and match.

1 **2** **3** **4** **5** **6**

4 CD2 19 20 **Listen and sing.**

Where animals live

6 Match the animals to where they live.

7 (Think!) **Make a poster.**

Thinking skills: Categorizing   **55**

7 I'm hungry!

1 ^{CD2}₂₅ Listen and point. Say the words.

1 carrots
2 sausages
3 apples
4 cakes
5 ice cream
6 fries

Chant → page 83

2 CD2 27 **Listen and circle ♡ or ⨂. Say the sentences.**

3 Listen and act. Listen and match.

1 **2** **3** **4** **5** **6**

4 CD2 30 31 **Listen and sing.**

Cakes and ice cream

Values

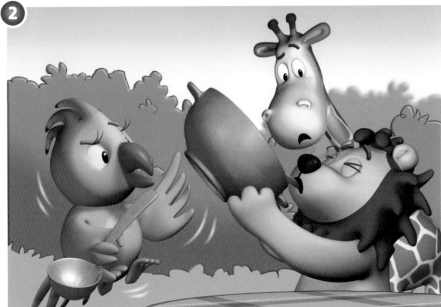

5

6

7

8

7

Family fun!

Value: Eating sensibly

Where food comes from

6 Match the food and where it comes from.

1
eggs

2
apples

3
carrots

4
milk

the ground

a cow

a chicken

a tree

7 (Think!) Make food collages.

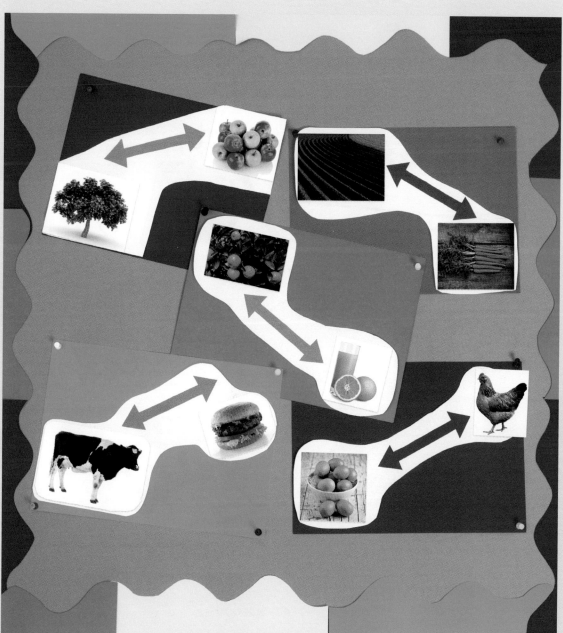

8 All aboard!

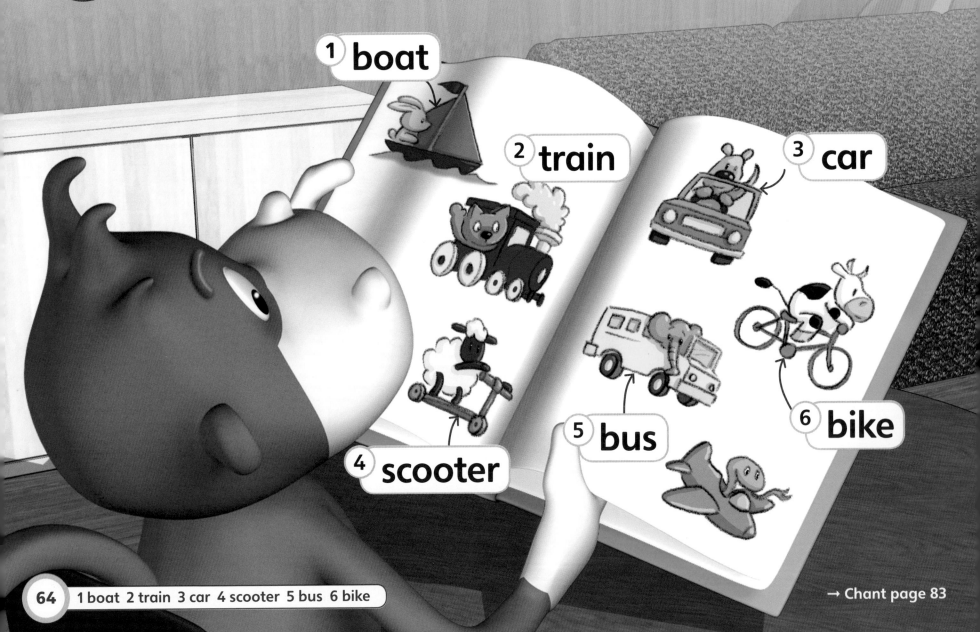

1 boat

2 train

3 car

4 scooter

5 bus

6 bike

→ Chant page 83

2 CD2 38 Listen and color. Act it out.

8

1

2

3

4

5

6

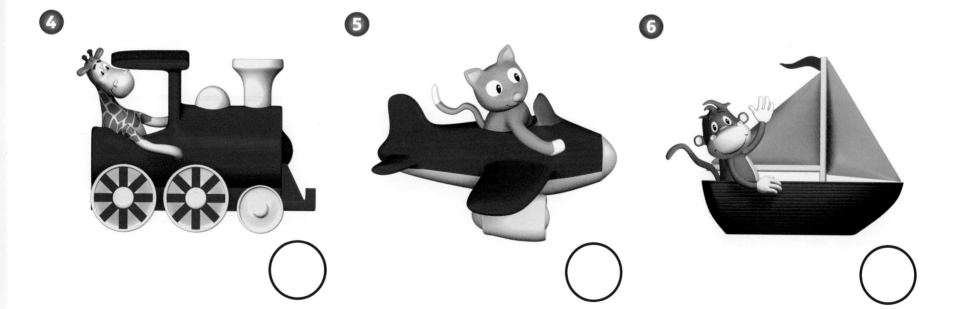

Family fun!

I'm / You're (riding) a (bike).

65

Listen and act. Listen and match.

1   **2**   **3**   **4**   **5**   **6**

4 CD2 42 43 Listen and sing.

5

6

7

8

Value: Saying *thank you*

Shape pictures

6 CD2 46 **Listen and color. Find shapes in the classroom.**

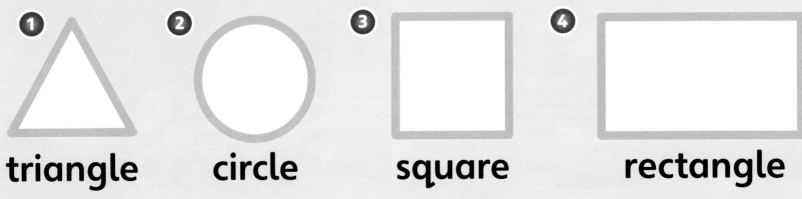

① triangle

② circle

③ square

④ rectangle

7 **Think!** **Count the shapes. Make a shapes picture.**

8

1

2

3

4

⑨ Party clothes

1 CD2 49 Listen and point. Say the words.

1 hat

2 belt

3 boots

4 shirt

5 button

6 shoes

1 hat 2 belt 3 boots 4 shirt 5 button 6 shoes

Chant → page 84

2 CD2 51 **Listen and point. Choose food for a class party.**

Family fun!

Let's have (cookies / chips / salad / candy).

Listen and act. Listen and match.

1 **2** **3** **4** **5** **6**

Total physical response

9

4 CD2 54 55 **Listen and sing.**

Nice work!

1

2

3

4

Our clothes

1 cowboy

2 superhero

3 pirate

4 princess

(Think!) **Listen and color. Look and color.**

1	2	3	4	5	6	7	8	9	10

1

CD1
08

  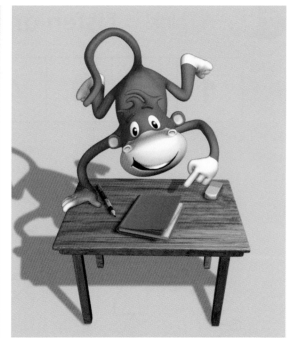

2

CD1
21

7

CD2 26

8

CD2 37

 1 CD1 18 **Listen and join in. Trace the letter.**

red

rabbit

 2 CD1 19 **Listen and read along.**

Rob the red rabbit, having fun, running in a race, run Rob run!

1 Listen and join in. Trace the letter.

fish

family

Four funny fish, swimming in the sea, four funny fish in the fish family

 2 Listen and read along.

1 **Listen and join in. Trace the letter.**

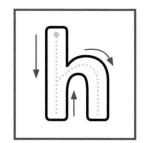

happy

hat

2 Listen and read along.

Hello!

I'm **H**arry the **h**orse,
I'm **h**appy today,
I've got my **h**at on my **h**ead,
let's go and play.

1 Listen and join in. Trace the letter.

dog

dig

**Gary's dog is very big,
Gary's dog likes to dig.**

2 Listen and read along.

1 CD2 12 **Listen and join in. Trace the letter.**

yellow

yogurt

Yummy yellow yogurt, yes yes yes!
Yummy yellow yogurt on my dress.

 2 CD2 13 **Listen and read along.**

1 Listen and join in. Trace the letter.

Z

zebra

zoo

**Zebra, zebra, at the zoo,
zebra, zebra, we love you!**

 2 Listen and read along.

1 CD2 34 **Listen and join in. Trace the letters.**

c

k

cat   king

**Cats and cakes and kites and bikes,
all the things that King Carl likes.**

2 CD2 35 **Listen and read along.**

1 **Listen and join in. Trace the letters.**

singing

dancing

We like singing, singing a song, singing and dancing, all day long.

 2 **Listen and read along.**

Listen and say. Trace the letters.

a   b    c

d    e    f    g

h    i    j

k    l    m    n

o

p

q

r

s

t

u

v

w

x

y

z

1 **Play the game.**

1 Play the game.

Page
102

1 **Play the game.**

1 Play the game.

✂ Page 102

1 **Play the game.**

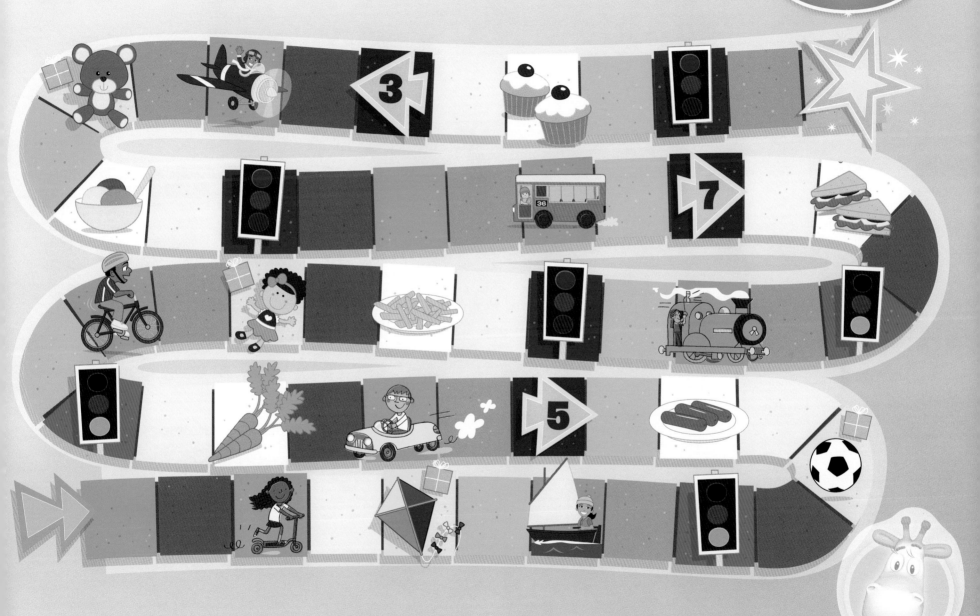

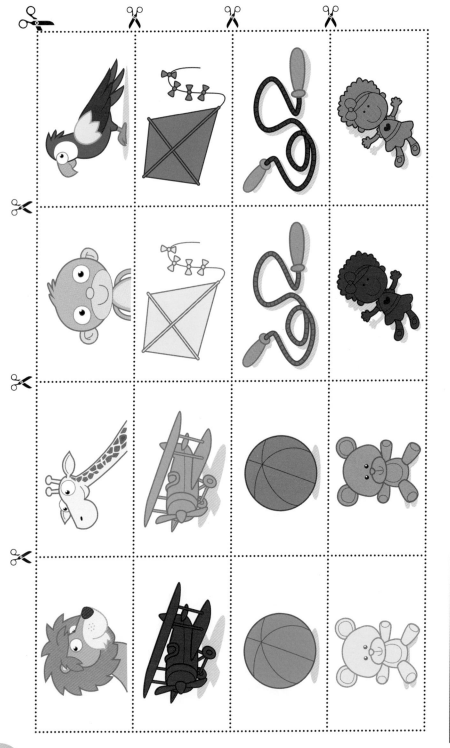

Good job!

....

has finished Super Safari!

Thanks and acknowledgments

Authors' thanks

The authors would like to thank a number of people who have made significant contributions towards the final form of Super Safari: Colin Sage, Helen Brock, and Carolyn Wright, our editors, for their expertise in working on the manuscripts, and the support we got from them.

Our designers, Blooberry, for their imaginative layout and all the artists – in particular Bill Bolton – for the inspiring artwork that has brought our ideas to life in such beautiful ways.

Liane Grainger, Managing Editor and Emily Hird, Publisher, for their many useful suggestions for improvement.

Jason Mann, Editorial Director at Cambridge University Press, for his vision and encouragement.

The publishers are grateful to the following contributors:

Blooberry Design: cover design, book design, publshing management and page make-up
Bill Bolton: cover illustration
Alison Prior: picture research
John Marshall Media: audio recording and production
James Richardson: chant writing and production
Robert Lee, Dib Dib Dub Studios: song writing and production
Lisa Hutchins: freelance editor

The publishers and authors are grateful to the following illustrators:

Peter Allen; Bill Bolton; John Haslam; Martin Lowe; Marek Jagucki; Maud Mondrimane (The Bright Agency); Theresa Tibbetts; Martin Sanders (Beehive); Kate Daubney

The authors and publishers acknowledge the following sources of copyright material and are grateful for the permissions granted. While every effort has been made, it has not always been possible to identify the sources of all the material used, or to trace all copyright holders. If any omissions are brought to our notice, we will be happy to include the appropriate acknowledgments on reprinting.

The publishers are grateful to the following for permission to reproduce copyright photographs and material:

p.15 (2): Shutterstock/© Zonefatal; p.15 (3): Shutterstock/© Marting Garnham; p.15 (4): Alamy/© Angela Hampton Picture Library; p.30 (TL): Shutterstock/© Elena Schweitzer; p.30 (TR): Shutterstock/© Tim Arbaev; p.30 (BL): iStockphoto/© Ju-Lee; p.30 (BR): Shutterstock/© Timmary; p.46 (I): iStockphoto/© onfilm; p.46 (2): Getty Images/© Riser/Andrea Pistolesi; p.46 (3): Shutterstock/©Songquan Deng; p.46 (4): Corbis/© Chris Rainier; p.46 (5): Shutterstock/© Serghei Starus; p.54 (TL): Shutterstock/© Rich Carey; p.54 (TCL, CL, BR, BL): Shutterstock/© Eric Isslee; p.54 (TR): Shutterstock/© Richard Peterson; p.54 (CR): Shutterstock/© Alexander Kazantsev; p.54 (BC): Shutterstock/© Sofia Santos; p.54 (T): Shutterstock/© Andrew Roland; p.54 (C): Shutterstock/© Galynn Andrusko; p.54 (B): Shutterstock/© Iakovfilimonov; p.62 (I): Shutterstock/© Paul Cowan; p.62 (2): Shutterstock/© Elena Schweitzer; p.62 (3): Shutterstock/© Lepas; p.62 (4): Shutterstock/© Eva Vargyasi; p.62 (ground): Shutterstock/© Peter Gudella; p.62 (cow): Shutterstock/© aleks.k; p.62 (chicken): Shutterstock/© ronfromyork; p.62 (tree): Shutterstock/© Bronwyn Photo; p.63 (tree): Shutterstock/© UKmooney; p.63 (apples): Shutterstock/© Steve Cukrov; p.63 (ground): Shutterstock/© Nevo; p.63 (carrots): Shutterstock/© Liligraphie; p.63 (orange tree): Shutterstock/© Jajaladdawan; p.63 (juice): Shutterstock/© Loskutnikov; p.63 (hen): Shutterstock/© Akesenova Natalya; p.63 (eggs): Shutterstock/© Maryloo; p.63 (cow): Shutterstock/© Eric Isselee; p.63 (burger): Shutterstock/© Kazoka

Commissioned photography on pp. 6, 15 (TL, TR, I, 5, 6), 23, 38, 39, 47, 49, 55, 63 (TL, BL), 70, 78, 95, 97, 98 by Stephen Bond